Introduction

Appreciation for antique quilts has grown over the past several decades. From their humble origins as bedspreads, quilts now grace museum walls and command impressive prices in auction rooms. After languishing for more than a century in dusty attics, these priceless heirlooms are now recognized for their beauty, graphic sophistication and outstanding craftsmanship.

The Whitney Museum of American Art in New York paid tribute to the cultural significance of quilts by mounting a major exhibition in 1971, "Abstract Design in American Quilts." Before this date, quilts were not considered a subject for art history. Today their use of abstract designs, repeating geometric patterns and bold color are seen as part of the design tradition that has inspired the modern art movements of the 1950s, '60s and '70s. Exhibitions like the one at the Whitney successfully opened the eyes of thousands who had never dreamed that a quilt could become such a highly valued collectible.

Quilts have also been revalued at a grassroots level. In 1982, the first American state quilt project was initiated by quilters and quilt-lovers in Kentucky who set out to document the history of quiltmaking in their state. The success of their findings spawned a nationwide movement to search out and catalog America's quiltmaking heritage. Thousands upon thousands of old quilts surfaced to be photographed and documented. North Carolina alone now has a permanent record of over ten thousand quilts. These findings have become invaluable historical and social documents of America's past, as well as an encyclopaedic source of information for quilt enthusiasts. Inspired by the excitement generated by America's "quilt hunt," quilt-lovers in other countries have embarked on similar ventures of discovery.

A quilt is simply two layers of material with padding between, held together with stitches. The quilt top is traditionally decorative, either appliquéd (a design created by adding layers of fabric on top of one another) or constructed of pieces of cloth sewn together.

The technique for making quilted cloth goes back to the Egyptians and was introduced into Europe at the end of the eleventh century by the Crusaders, returning from the Holy Wars. They had adopted the Eastern style of quilted fabric armor. Worn under metal armor it provided cushioning and protection from the rough metal work, while for the poorer soldier it was a cheap and lightweight form of armor.

As bedcoverings, quilts date back to the fourteenth century. Although there are earlier references to quilts in literature, wills and household inventories, the earliest existing examples are a pair made in Sicily for the marriage of members of the Guicciardini and Acciaiuili families in 1395. Made of linen with wool lining, they have been quilted in brown linen thread with scenes from the life of Tristram.

In the following centuries both quilted garments and quilted bedcovers became increasingly popular and appear frequently in inventories of wealthy households. In 1592 Carew Castle in Wales lists -

"Item ij old quiltes of yellow sernet, xxs.
Item a changeable silke quilt, price xxs.
Item an old black and white silke quilt for a bedd, price iijs."

Catherine Howard, fifth wife of Henry VIII, was given 23 quilts as a mark of favor in 1540.

In the seventeenth century, colorful and colorfast chintzes from India arrived in Britain. These glazed cotton chintzes, often featuring large birds and exotic plants, popularized quiltmaking. The

QUILTS

Ljiljana Baird

Museum Quilts Publications

Published by Museum Quilts (UK) Inc.
254-258 Goswell Road
London EC1V 7EB

Copyright © 1994 Museum Quilts Publications, Inc.
Text © 1994 Ljiljana Baird

9 8 7 6 5 4 3 2 1
Digit on the right indicates the number of this printing

ISBN 1-897954-28-X

A CIP catalogue record of this book
is available from the British Library

Typeset in Baskerville
Printed in Korea

emphasis moved from decorative quilting patterns to the application of figurative chintz motifs onto a solid ground. This technique became known as broderie perse.

After the seventeenth century the story of quiltmaking shifts to America. The tradition arrived with the early British settlers, and in a very short time disparate ethnic groups had adopted quiltmaking as their primary form of bedding for everyday use and for special occasions.

The first quilts made in America were modeled on the whole-cloth (a one-piece top with decorative stitching) and medallion styles (a quilt with a central panel surrounded by a series of borders). A third early eighteenth-century quiltmaking option consisted of four large blocks, roughly 36 inches square, to which a wide border was added. It is from this model that the block quilt, as we know it today, emerged. Whether for portability, economy or ease of working smaller units, nineteenth-century quiltmakers experimented with progressively smaller blocks. This functional technique, developed in America in the early 1800s, became the quiltmaker's favorite method of quilt construction.

The seventy quilts featured in this book represent a chronological glimpse into the past two hundred years of quiltmaking, a treasure house of colorful quilts with even more colorful names. Starting with a silk embroidered coverlet made in Ireland in 1712, and ending with an American Yo-yo quilt of the 1930s, these quilts offer a tantalizing introduction to a remarkable textile heritage.

$\mathcal{M}$ARTHA LENNOX, DAUGHTER OF JOHN HAMILTON, the first Sovereign (Mayor) of Belfast, made this delicate floral quilt in 1712. Worked on cream linen, it combines outstanding embroidery work with decorative background quilting. In her design Martha Lennox displays great artistry, combining influences from Oriental textiles with a delicately observed English naturalism. The brilliantly colored embroidery is executed in a variety of stitches—satin stitch, stem stitch, french knots and laidwork. Through her skilled use of colors, sometimes combining three or four shades of one color, she achieves a rich painterly effect. The quilt top, a fine, cream-colored linen, is attached to a coarser linen backing. There is no interlining. She has used pale green French silk to quilt an overall diamond pattern in an extraordinarily even half inch grid. This background quilting is done as a "fill-in" after the embroidery is finished.

The quilt has been passed down through the female line of the family. A letter from Martha McTier, who inherited the quilt in 1800, reveals that her forebear Martha Lennox spent £30 on French embroidery twist to stitch her quilt "—the coloured silks it is wrought in cost £30." In the eighteenth century this was a vast sum of money, more than the yearly wage of a manual laborer.

The Lennox Quilt
signed and dated: "Martha Lennox," 1712, Ireland
72 x 78 inches
Courtesy The Ulster Museum, Belfast, Northern Ireland

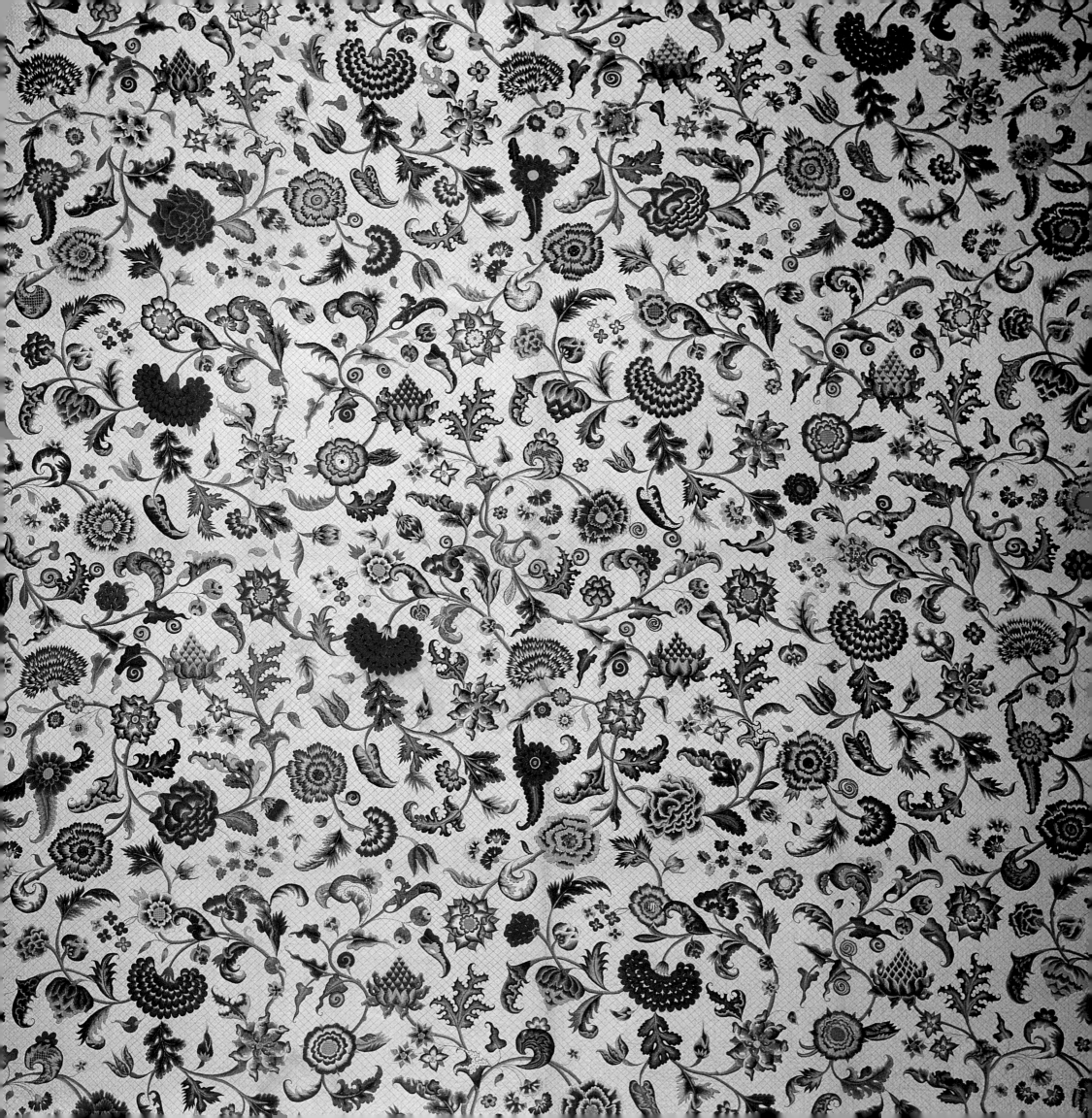

*T*his is a wonderful example of eighteenth-century inlay work and comes from the border area of southeastern Germany.

Inlay is a technique more commonly associated with decorative woodwork, but this quilt applies the same principles to fabric. Each piece of the design is cut away from the host fabric and replaced with an exact piece in a different color. This work requires great precision to achieve a perfect result —the locking together of the two fabrics without overlapping or spaces. The joining is often done with an overcast stitch on the right side which is then covered with cord. The pencil thin lines on this quilt have been achieved by sewing thin strips sideways on (so that the pile of the fabric is facing outwards) between two pieces of fabric.

This heraldic quilt has been pieced from regimental cloths and assorted velvet scraps. It carries an exotic assortment of geometric patterns and pictorial images. Foot-soldiers, sabre-bearing Turks, swash-buckling cavalry, hunters, tight-rope walkers and turban-clad Orientals smoking long pipes make a colorful parade around the borders.

Eighteenth-century Inlay Quilt
1776-1779, southeastern Germany
77 x 95 inches
Courtesy The Bautzen City Museum, Bautzen, Germany

QUILTING IN THE EARLY PART OF THE EIGHTEENTH CENTURY WAS CONSIDERED AS AN ARM OF EMBROIDERY, and in this coverlet the two disciplines work together beautifully. It was made by, or under the instruction of, Lady Helena McDonnell (1705-1783), sister of the 5th Earl of Antrim.

Bedding of this magnificence was the luxury of royalty and nobility. Poorer households did not have the means for rich fabrics and expensive silk thread, nor did they have the time to work such ornate designs. Probably made as a wedding gift, the coverlet is part of a set which includes valances, a cushion, pillow and bolster covers.

On a canvas of ivory silk an elaborate floral medallion with an unusual garland border has been embroidered in a variety of stitches. It has been executed with such skill as to appear three dimensional, with the leaves achieving a rich velvety depth. The background has been densely stitched in gold thread, in an overall vermicular pattern. This serpentine background pattern, a much admired feature on coverlets brought back from the Far East, was adopted by English needlewomen. It is sometimes referred to as "pseudo quilting" because the stitch does not fasten all three layers together. On the Antrim Coverlet the stitching passes through the satin top and is secured to a coarse linen lining. It is backed with tissue-thin ivory-colored silk.

Antrim Bed Furniture
18th century, Ireland
60 x 62 inches
Courtesy The Ulster Museum, Belfast, Northern Ireland

English Feather Medallion
c.1790, England
85 x 85 inches
Courtesy The Antique Textile Company, London, England

*T*HE OVAL CENTERPIECE OF FOUR OSTRICH FEATHERS ON A YELLOW GROUND is an example of eighteenth-century English block printing, the earliest form of textile printing. A design is carved in relief on a wooden block, each color in the design requiring a separate block. The blocks are in turn pressed against a dye-saturated woolen sieve and then applied to the cloth. A solid blow with a mallet to the back of the block transfers the design. Different designs required the blocks to be made from different wood—holly and boxwood were suitable for small-scale, finely detailed patterns; walnut and lime for large-scale prints.

The oval centerpiece is framed with a printed ric-rac braid and is set on a woven Scottish shawl fabric.

The Austen Quilt
1811, Chawton, Hampshire, England
80 x 112 inches
Courtesy The Jane Austen Memorial Trust, Chawton, England

THIS CHARMING ENGLISH QUILT WAS MADE IN 1811 BY JANE AUSTEN, her sister Cassandra and her mother at Chawton, where Jane spent her last eight years. In a letter dated 1811 to her sister, Jane enquires after the quilt, "Have you collected the pieces for the patchwork?"

By the nineteenth century, quiltmaking was an established form of needlework throughout all classes of English society. The arrival of the colorful and colorfast chintz fabrics from India helped to popularize the vogue for quiltmaking among the middle classes.

The Austen quilt is an unusual version of the medallion style—a diamond-shaped, chintz flower basket is surrounded by a pattern of repeating diamonds. They are cut from a selection of delicate chintz fabrics and bordered by a black and white polka-dot print.

*T*HIS CRIB SIZE SUMMER COVERLET IS FULL OF CHARMING, youthful appeal and may have been made by a child. Its naive appliqué shapes, cut without a template (a rigid shape which can be traced around), are reminiscent of a child's scrap book. Two of each motif—scissors, crowns, sheep, birds, butterflies, dogs, stars, crescent moons and quatrefoils—have been arranged symmetrically around the central flower basket, under which are appliquéd the initials "A•R" and the date 1835. The linen top is finished with a progressive series of scrap borders pieced with triangles, squares and diamonds. On either side of the two flowerpots are two barely visible triangular shapes which have faded badly over the years.

Appliqué Summer Cover
signed and dated: "A•R,"1835, New England
49 x 51 inches
From the Barbara Horvath Collection, Switzerland

*T*HE NINE-PATCH DESIGN IS A SIMPLE PATTERN, popular with the novice and experienced quilter alike; for the novice because it is simple to cut and piece, and for the experienced quilter because it is the basis of many more difficult patterns.

The nine-patch blocks in this glorious eighteenth-century quilt are sewn to plain, unpieced blocks. This creates the horizontal and vertical grid. The quilting divides the unpieced squares into nine compartments.

The fabrics are a mixture of glazed chintz furnishing and dress fabrics. The wide border is a magnificent example of an English copperplate printed fabric. This method involved wiping dye across an incised copperplate and then transferring the design onto cloth. This technique prompted a new design style, the scenic toile, which depicted finely engraved images designed by artists.

Early Nine-patch Quilt
Early 1800s, USA
92 x 102 inches
Museum Quilts Gallery, London, England

$\mathcal{A}$N ALBUM QUILT, LIKE AN AUTOGRAPH ALBUM, is a record of many hands declaring their respect and good opinion of the owner. It is a co-operative effort where many separately designed and sewn blocks are assembled to make a finished quilt that would be presented to an individual, as a testimonial of the group's esteem.

The blocks are generally appliquéd (although some pieced album quilts do exist) with pictorial motifs cut from chintz fabric and further embellished with embroidery work. The most common motifs include flowers, baskets, fruit, wreaths and roses, birds and butterflies, bibles, anchors and eagles. Frequently a block would carry a hand-written or embroidered dedication, or just the contributor's name.

During the period 1840-1860, three types of Album quilts were immensely popular: Presentation Quilts, Friendship Quilts and Bride's Album Quilts. They reached their height of beauty and technical excellence in the famous Baltimore Album quilts.

On this highly ornate album quilt, six of the blocks have been inscribed in indelible ink with the contributors' names. Two blocks carry a short verse; Alice A. Ryder leaves this sentiment:

"Thy beauty is as undenied
As the beauty of a star
And thy heart beats just as equally
Whate'er thy praises are,
And so long without a parallel
Thy loveliness hath shone
That followed like the tided moon
Thou movest as calmly on"

The Baltimore Bride Quilt
signed and dated: "Alice A. Ryder," April 1st, 1847, Baltimore, Maryland
122 x 122 inches
Courtesy The American Museum in Britain, Claverton Manor, Bath, England

THE WORD PALAMPORE REFERS TO A PAINTED, dyed and glazed cotton bedcover made in India and imported into England during the late seventeenth and eighteenth centuries. The design is of a central, flowering tree on a single chintz panel. Europe was entranced by the brilliant and exotic appearance of this new printed textile. Chintz, to the detriment of all other European textiles, became the foremost dress and furnishing fabric for almost a hundred years.

This palampore was made for the Great Exhibition in Paris in 1855. Stylistically, it is a late example of this type of bedcover and features many Western preferences, especially obvious in the use of heavy swag borders and bows. Two outer borders of British block-printed furnishing cotton have been added, and it was probably quilted at the same time. Palampores were imported as one-piece bedcovers and were quilted later by the purchaser.

Palampore
c. 1853, India
130 x 104 inches
Courtesy Sarah Franklyn, London, England

*T*HIS CHEERFUL RED AND GREEN APPLIQUÉ QUILT, made before the American Civil War, exudes a great sense of warmth and security. The maker has used symbolic motifs that express permanence, freedom and well-being—schoolhouses flanked by the great Charter Oak create a border around the bountiful harvest wreaths.

The one-room schoolhouse, a significant American symbol, came to represent stability and respectability at a time when living conditions were primitive and often dangerous. Legend has it that the Colonial Charter of Connecticut was hidden in the Great White Oak of Hartford when James II demanded its surrender to the Dominion of New England.

Red and Green Floral Appliqué
c.1850, Pennsylvania
86 x 86 inches
Museum Quilts Gallery, London, England

*T*HE TUMBLING BLOCK PATTERN HAS SEVERAL DIFFERENT CONFIGURATIONS, and each is achieved by the arrangement of color and the placement of light and dark. The Stairway to Heaven pattern reads as steps converging into a V-shape; a three-dimensional looking Lone Star pattern is formed by converging triangles made up of cube shapes.

This Victorian Tumbling Blocks pattern incorporates a center diamond-shaped medallion. It has been achieved by creating a cross shape with four like-blocks, and to this is added a different ring of twelve blocks and then a final set of twenty blocks. This creates the diamond shape that stands out from the rest of the pattern. The maker has cleverly introduced a soft floral pattern to define the outer diamond shape.

Red and Black Tumbling Blocks
c.1850, New England
63 x 72 inches
From the Betsey Telford Collection, Colorado

*T*HIS EXCITING TEXTILE PICTURE WAS MADE BY TAILOR JAMES WILLIAMS over a period of ten years, using a technique of inlay. It is a form of appliqué in which the shapes and patterns are cut out from the main fabric and replaced by different colored fabrics. The work is a marvelous design of pictorial detail and abstract geometric patterns. The picture is composed asymmetrically, reminiscent of the way in which a crazy quilt is constructed. Using a dazzling array of colorful regimental facing cloths and felted cloth, the quilter has created a wealth of different geometric border patterns. The central scenes depict the stories of Adam in the Garden of Eden, Jonah and the Whale, Cain and Abel and Noah and the Ark. Among these Biblical scenes Williams includes pictorial representations of local engineering achievements such as the Menai suspension Bridge at Telford and the Cefn viaduct near Ruabon.

Pictorial Quilt
made by James Williams, 1852, Wrexham, Clwyd, Wales
82 x 90 inches
Courtesy The Welsh Folk Museum, St. Fagans, Wales

THIS LOVELY MID-NINETEENTH-CENTURY APPLIQUÉ COVERLET, filled with motifs associated with marriage such as the Rose of Sharon and the Rose Wreath, suggest that it was made as a wedding gift. The initials of the bride and groom are pieced rather ambiguously in each corner, giving us several possible readings. Pieced lettering is a distinctive characteristic of nineteenth-century quilts from the New York, New Jersey and Connecticut area. The sinuous and leafy quality of the appliquéd vine that runs the length of the border and along the sashing is echoed in the choice and expression of the blocks. The quilt has a verdant freshness that has been achieved by the use of color and the delicate appliqué work. The third row of blocks has a particular elegance that stands out from the rest and indicates that there were probably several contributors to the quilt.

Album Coverlet
c.1850, New York State
76 x 86 inches
From the Martha Jackson Collection, Vermont

*T*HE STAR PATTERN OUTNUMBERS ALL OTHER PATTERNS IN POPULARITY. It has been used repeatedly throughout the history of quiltmaking and the variations are seemingly endless. As well as representing a hopeful and romantic image, the star pattern presents a needlework challenge.

Most stars are constructed from diamond shaped pieces. Cutting and sewing these acute angles with precision requires great skill. Like a jigsaw puzzle all the pieces must fit precisely together, and any variation will throw the whole pattern out. Countless Lone Star quilt tops exist unfinished because of error.

This version is a highly individual interpretation of a central star. The "Lone Star" refers to the State of Texas. Both the Republic and the idea of a single star designed to cover the whole top of a bed, were born at around the same time. One hundred small, eight-pointed stars, called Le Moyne stars after the founding fathers of New Orleans, move as a galaxy around the central image.

Stars
1855, Texas
88 x 94 inches
Private Collection

THIS EXQUISITELY SEWN NINETEENTH-CENTURY QUILT presents a unique treatment of several very old piecing and appliqué patterns. The central intersecting pink and green cross is a Wild Goose Chase, an early pattern dating back to the first half of the eighteenth century. The currants form a cruciform on top and the showy coxcombs sweep across the composition like oriental feathered fans.

The quilt has been executed in the favorite palette of nineteenth-century appliqué quiltmakers—red and green with accents of bright pink and yellow on a white background. The reason for this color preference is unknown. However, these fabrics held their color with good reliability and since an appliqué quilt was most frequently intended as a "best" quilt (brought out for special occasions, or made as a gift) it made sense to use fabrics that would not ruin a labor of love, which would have taken many years to complete.

Coxcomb and Currant Variation
c.1850, Peewee Valley, Kentucky
75 x 80 inches
Museum Quilts Gallery, London, England

Medallion Sampler
c.1850, Pennsylvania
84 x 84 inches
Courtesy Aly Goodwin
The N. E. Horton Antique Quilt Collection, North Carolina

A SAMPLER QUILT IS OFTEN MADE AS A TEACHING OR LEARNING QUILT. Here a novice quilter may practice her skills on a variety of different piecing and appliqué patterns. For the experienced quiltmaker, samplers offer an opportunity to experiment with different blocks and techniques without committing the time needed to make many quilts.

In this early sampler, twenty-eight blocks have been sewn onto a foundation cloth. The large sun, made from many radiating bands of small triangles, and the four tulip pots have been appliquéd onto the foundation. It is an unusual composition of a large central cross and four smaller ones.

This quilt was found incomplete and unquilted. In 1990 its present owner commissioned Elreda Johnson of Colorado to quilt it with a variety of traditional patterns.

Rebecca Temperley's Quilt
made by Rebecca Temperley, 1860
Allendale, Northumberland, England
108 x 108 inches
Courtesy The Bowes Museum, Barnard Castle, Co. Durham, England

THIS WONDERFUL AND HIGHLY ORIGINAL QUILT WAS MADE by Rebecca Temperley of Allendale, Northumberland in the 1860s as part of her wedding trousseau. Family lore has it that she wished it to be inherited by the first granddaughter to be named after her.

Fashioned from popular dress prints of the period, this quilt combines piecing and appliqué with traditional North Country quilting patterns. The central panel includes motifs usually associated with marriage—a 16-point star, four hearts and four "lucky" clover leaves, curved leafy sprays with pears, and sprigs with birds. Its delicacy is reminiscent of an eighteenth-century filigree brooch. The quilting is finely worked in patterns which echo the appliqué motifs and the wide border displays an intricate arrangement of cables and diamonds enclosing clover shapes, hearts and leaves.

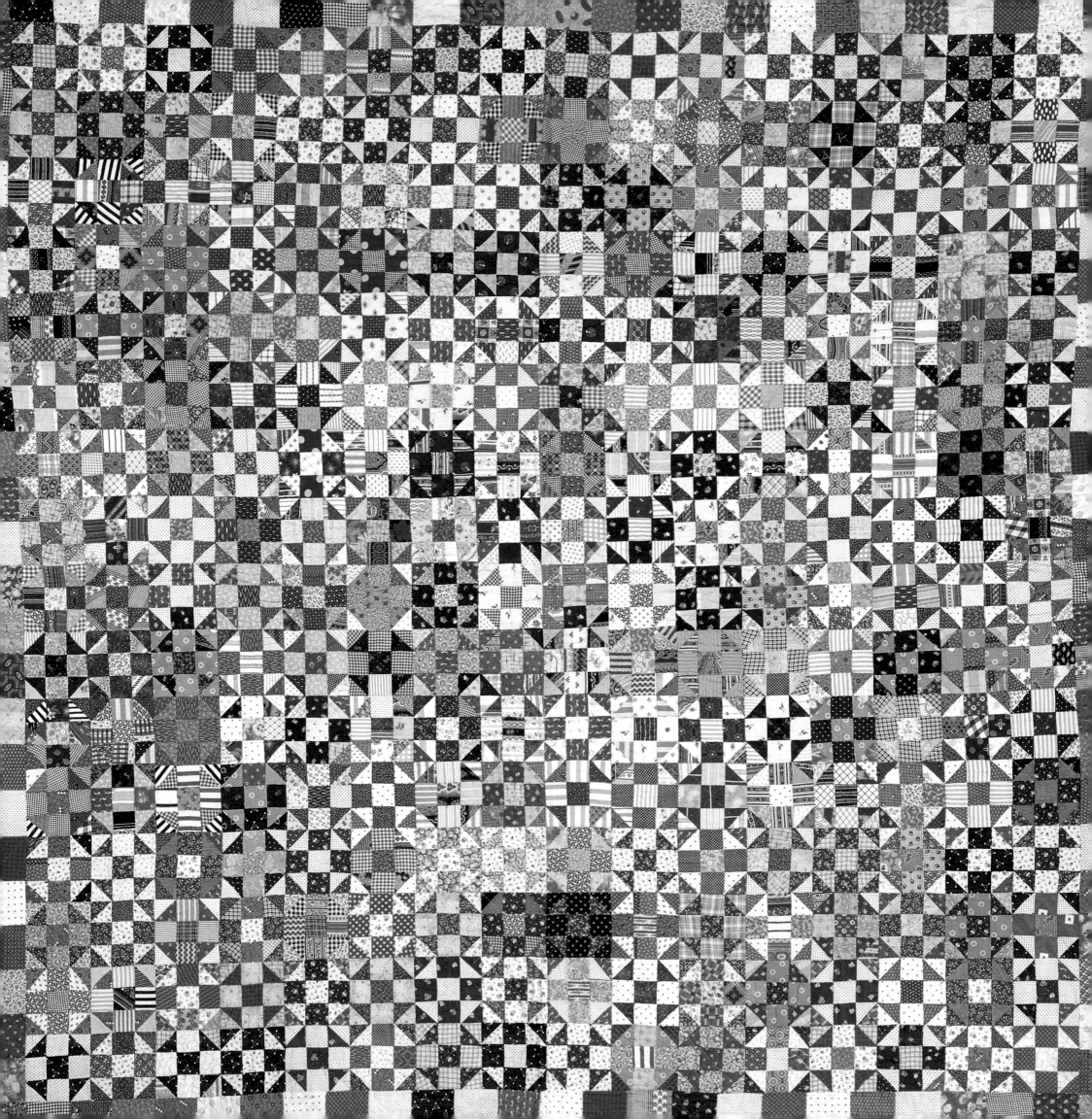

"Flies in the buttermilk shoo, fly, shoo

Flies in the buttermilk shoo, fly, shoo

Flies in the buttermilk shoo, fly, shoo

Skip to my Lou my darling."

*T*HIS QUILT TEEMS WITH VITALITY—LIKE A SWARM OF FLIES AROUND THE MILK POT. The name is also associated with the famous dessert, Shoo-fly Pie—a sticky, spiced cake with molasses which, being so sweet, attracts flies during baking.

The shoo-fly block is a simple nine-patch design, and in this variation the four corner blocks have been cut in half to make triangles. This gives the block its busy appearance and allows the maker to use even smaller pieces. This mid-nineteenth-century scrap quilt is a marvelous catalog of fabrics of the period.

In the early colonial days, fabrics were scarce and highly prized. Making homespun cloth was a long and arduous task, and there was barely enough to supply the needs of the family. This shortage was aggravated by England's ban on the direct import of fabric to America. The colonists were dependent on what England deemed appropriate to export. Consequently the practice of saving all fabric remnants and the recycling of worn garments was assiduously undertaken by women at all social and economic levels.

Shoo-fly
c.1860, USA
72 x 72 inches
Museum Quilts Gallery, London, England

QUILT PATTERN NAMES CAN PROVIDE US WITH AN INTERESTING RECORD of public interest and sentiments on numerous issues.

From the political dispute during the 1840s between the Whigs and the Democrats, two new quilt patterns—the Whig Rose and the Democrat Rose—emerged, with each party claiming their own. The dispute was resolved at the 1844 Presidential election with the defeat of the Whig candidate Henry Clay by the Democrat James K. Polk. From Clay's demise sprang a new pattern name—Whig's Defeat.

The stories of many a politician or military figure are similarly immortalized in a pattern name—Garfield's Monument, Clay's Choice, Burgoyne Surrounded and Lincoln's Platform.

Whig's Defeat
c.1860, Georgia
90 x 93 inches
Museum Quilts Gallery, London, England

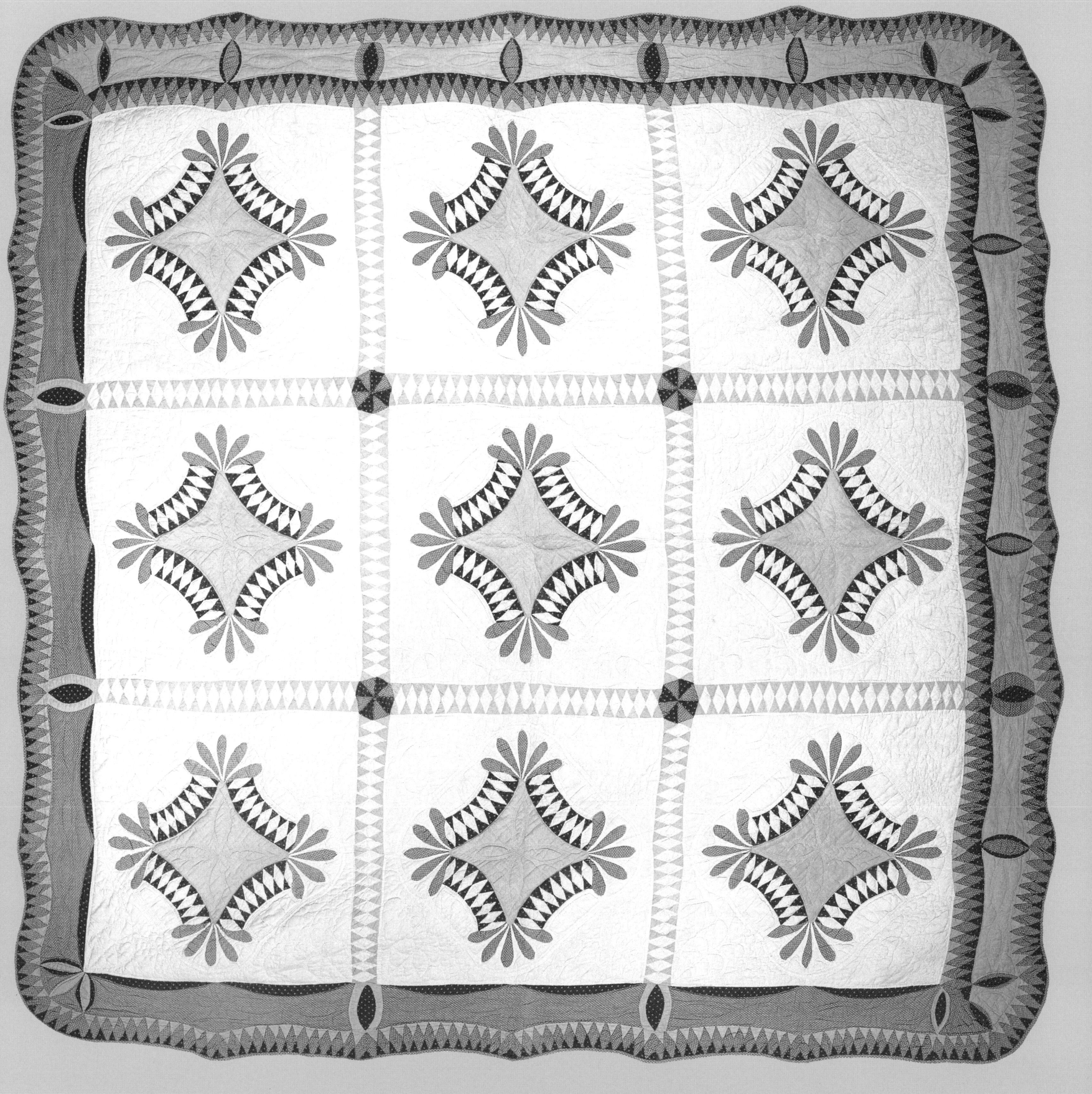

ENNSYLVANIA DUTCH (a corruption of the word Deutsch, meaning German) quilts are filled with joyful folk images and motifs, recalling memories—real or imagined—of the makers' ancestral German homeland. Worked in lively shades of red, green and yellow with abundant patches of brightly patterned calico, these quilts are an affirmation of the optimism of the German settlers.

This mid-nineteenth-century quilt, which incorporates appliqué, piecing, reverse appliqué and embroidered cording on a bright acid green background, has the decorative qualities of the gingerbread house found by Hansel and Gretel. The oak leaf is the favored motif. It is worked around the border and in the body of the quilt, evoking the canopy of an ancient oak wood. Even the fabrics chosen carry the theme. Among the German-speaking countries, the oak is a popular and cherished symbol of longevity and fertility.

Pennsylvania Dutch Folk Art Appliqué
c.1860, Pennsylvania
72 x 92 inches
Museum Quilts Gallery, London, England

$\mathcal{T}$AKING INTO ACCOUNT THE DATE ON THE QUILT and the possible significance of the arc of thirteen stars above the Federal Eagle, we can surmise that it was made to celebrate the Thirteenth Amendment to the American Constitution—

"Neither slavery nor involuntary servitude, except as a punishment for crime whereof the party shall have been duly convicted, shall exist within the United States, or any place subject to their jurisdiction."

The design has been beautifully conceived and follows an early quilt construction technique of appliquéing the central motifs onto four large blocks. In this case, the English poppy design makes up the central square.

Floral Appliqué with Eagles and Stars
1865, Roosevelt, Ohio
80 x 80 inches
From the Shelly Zegart Collection, Kentucky

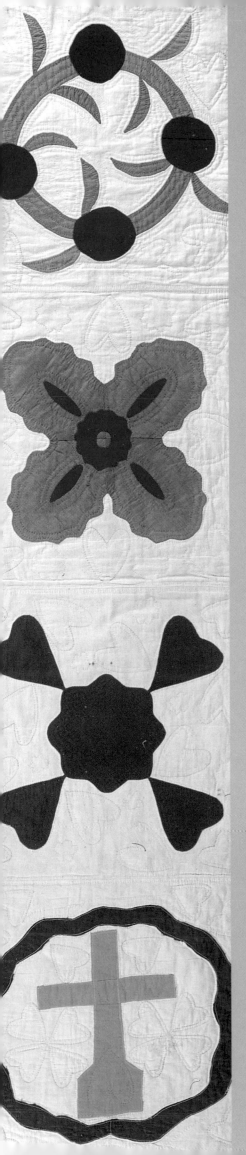

*T*HIS ALBUM QUILT WAS MADE BY AT LEAST FIVE DIFFERENT HANDS. Dellia Howell, S. Howell, Ida Weller and E.M. Rutland have each signed their blocks with pencil. The fifth contributor is Mary E. Rutland, whom we know was an African-American woman from the Smithville district of Brunswick County, North Carolina. She has embroidered her name prominently in red thread across the chalice, which suggests that she may have been the principal maker.

The Rutland quilt uses motifs that can be found on other white album quilts of the same period—oak leaves, wreaths, hearts, and the Rose of Sharon. However, it does not share the same representational realism or heady, decorative sweetness. The appliquéd blocks made from solid work-a-day fabrics are strong, simplified images. The inclusion of such items as cooking pots and soup kettles, cotton balls, hearts, pomegranates and the distinctly religious icons of crosses, a crown of thorns, an olive tree and a communal chalice reveal much about the preoccupation and social status of the makers. The distinctive emblematic quality of this quilt gives it the appearance of a contemporary church banner.

Album Quilt
signed: "Mary E. Rutland"
c.1860, North Carolina
78 x 84 inches
Museum Quilts Gallery, London, England

— 45 —

$\mathcal{G}$ENERALLY SPEAKING, QUILTMAKING HAS BEEN AND CONTINUES to be a female activity. Men may have assisted in the art—by cutting fabric or designing and building quilting frames—but they have rarely participated in the actual piecing or quilting.

From the large number of similar patchwork quilts made by soldiers exhibited for the 1890 Royal Military Exhibition at the Chelsea Hospital in London, it can be safely assumed that this amazing mosaic quilt was worked by a man. Thousands of half-inch woolen squares, cut from regimental uniforms, have been pieced together in a variety of configurations to make up twenty-five blocks. They are contained within a frame of smaller squares and finished with a zig-zag border. The predominance of scarlet indicates that the quilt was made after 1872, when scarlet would have been plentiful, and probably before 1881 when the facing colors for Infantry were limited to white, yellow, green and navy blue.

Military Patchwork
c.1870s, England
72 x 76 inches
Museum Quilts Gallery, London, England

A CIRCLE WITH RADIATING POINTS IS AN OLD QUILT PATTERN, thought to have evolved from the wind roses found on compass points and sea charts. The earliest known quilts bearing this pattern are English, and date back to the eighteenth century.

This elegant variation of the Mariner's Compass has been pieced using an array of nineteenth-century printed cottons in a distinguished palette of brown and red with accents of pink, white and green. It is a difficult pattern to construct because it requires accurate cutting and piecing of sharp, narrow points.

Mariner's Compass
c.1860, New York State
67 x 87 inches
Museum Quilts Gallery, London, England

The Irish Chain pattern can be pieced as a Single, Double or Triple chain. The Single Irish Chain is a variation of the nine-patch block. The nine-patch block is assembled from a single, plain color. To each corner is appliquéd a small square, the color of the chain. These additional second colored squares cause the nine-patch pattern to recede, and the chain pattern to dominate.

The restrained and sober quality of this two-colored quilt suggests that it may have been made as a mourning quilt by the bereaved. The dart motif signifying the "black darts of death" is used as part of the swag border.

Single Irish Chain
c. 1870, Virginia
79 x 79 inches
From the Barbara Horvath Collection, Switzerland

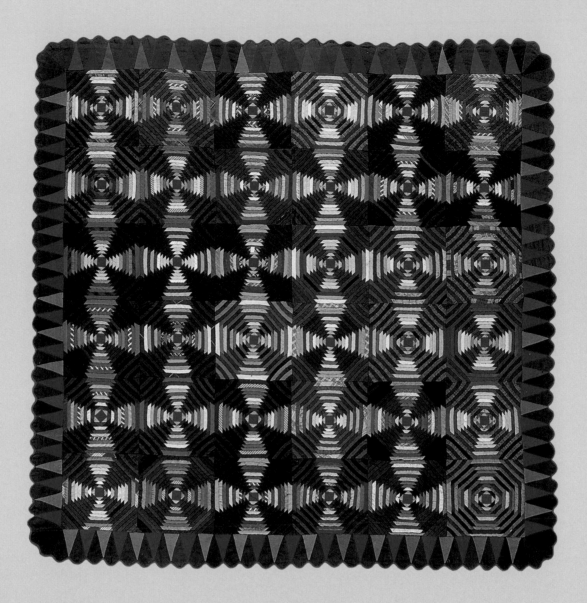

Log Cabin, Pineapple Variation
c.1870, Kentucky
70 x 70 inches
Museum Quilts Gallery, London, England

THE LOG CABIN AS A QUILT PATTERN NAME is mentioned in literature of the 1860s and may have been inspired by Abraham Lincoln's presidential campaign of 1860. In a call for order and decency, he used the log cabin as a symbol of the virtues attached to simple country living.

The pineapple motif is used in both appliqué and pieced quilts and is a symbol of hospitality. The Pineapple variation of the Log Cabin design is an extremely complicated pieced pattern, and unraveling the mystery of its making is a near impossibility. The juxtaposition of light and dark shapes in this challenging quilt moves the eye through a series of changing patterns from four-pointed stars to interlocking circles, bulls-eyes and windmill sails. All of these visual illusions conspire to distance the observer from how the quilt was made.

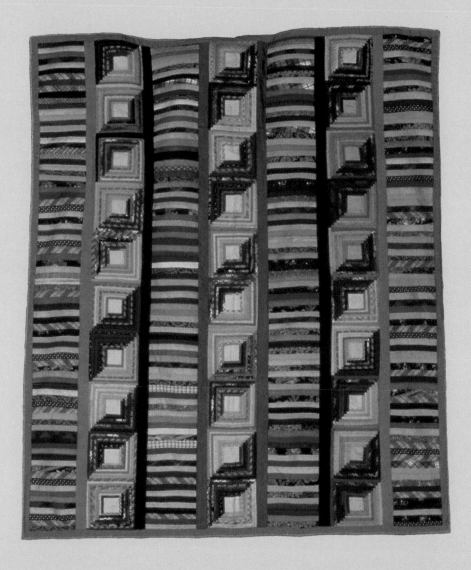

Roman Stripe Log Cabin
c.1860, Massachusetts
62 x 76 inches
From the Betsey Telford Collection, Colorado

THIS IS AN ORIGINAL STRIP QUILT DESIGN INCORPORATING two popular quilt patterns, both of which use narrow strips in their construction. The Roman Stripe is a series of parallel bands sewn together to make a long column, and the Log Cabin pattern is created by sewing narrow strips around a small central square. In this quilt the two patterns are presented in alternating columns. The dominant vertical thrust of the design is foiled by a masterful use of the dark diagonal furrows in the Log Cabin pattern.

Both of these patterns are ideal for making scrap quilts, as the small log-like strips can be constructed from fabric scraps too small for other patterns.

*S*KETCHY PROVENANCE ON THIS QUILT suggests that it was made out of ball gowns and fancy dresses from a family in Louisville, Kentucky. It is a glorious optical illusion of patterned and plain silks.

The game of visual deception, of making what is two dimensional appear three dimensional, has engaged mankind since the Egyptians. The Victorians were fascinated by optical illusion and incorporated the principles into their quiltmaking.

Depending on how you view this quilt, the blocks change from appearing like an opened concertina of postcards to blocks that seem to radiate from the center of the quilt.

The tumbling block is a one-patch design, curiously formed from three diamond-shaped pieces rather than from squares. The three-dimensional effect is achieved by careful placement of light and dark—usually a dark colored diamond is sewn to a medium colored diamond, and then a light one is added to complete the block.

Silk Tumbling Blocks
c.1870, USA
74 x 75 inches
Museum Quilts Gallery, London, England

*R*EVERSE APPLIQUÉ IS A TECHNIQUE in which several different colored layers of fabric are first basted together, after which designs are cut through from the top to reveal the layers beneath. The cut edges are turned under and invisibly hemmed. The next layers are handled in the same way. Reverse appliqué as a needlework technique is used by many different cultures, notably by the Hmong people of South East Asia and the San Blas Indians of Panama in their decorative "molas."

This elegant floral quilt uses an unusual color scheme of vermilion, pink and yellow. The linear arrangement of the floral motifs with the vertical run of diamonds gives the quilt a strong sense of movement. It has been beautifully finished with an elaborate saw-tooth border that is also used to define the diamond shapes.

Floral Reverse Appliqué
c.1870, Vermont
82 x 86 inches
Museum Quilts Gallery, London, England

$\mathcal{T}$he Centennial celebrations in America in 1876 produced a burst of creative energy on all levels of art, craft and needlework. Quilts with patriotic motifs abounded, and fabrics specially printed with flags, eagles, national heroes, prominent buildings and events were manufactured for quiltmakers.

This quilt, appliquéd in red and green on a white ground was made for the 1876 Centennial Exhibition in Philadelphia. It has as its central motif the Federal Eagle (copied from the Great Seal of America) flanked by two diminutive songbirds. Ten wheels with spokes of carnation stems surround the three birds.

There is a refreshing lack of uniformity to the appliqué pieces. They have been cut without a template—each carnation stem is different from the next, the central rosettes are of different shape and size, and the saw-tooth border is as unique as any mountain range. Beautifully quilted with interlocking clamshells, this quilt radiates a simple and generous patriotism.

Centennial Eagle
c.1876, Philadelphia
70 x 88 inches
Museum Quilts Gallery, London, England

Underground Railroad
c.1870, USA
90 x 90 inches
Museum Quilts Gallery, London, England

THE RESONANCE OF THE BITTER DEBATE ON SLAVERY is felt in the naming of this quilt. The "underground railroad" was an organization of individuals who helped spirit black fugitives to the safety of the North. Its pre-Civil War name was Jacob's Ladder, and in other parts of America it is variously known as Stepping Stones, The Tail of Benjamin's Kite, Trail of the Covered Wagon and Wagon Tracks.

This two-color quilt is a rather simple nine-patch construction of thirty-six blocks. However, the finished appearance is one of considerable complexity. The overwhelmingly strong diagonal thrust dominates its square construction and requires the viewer's concentration to "see" the nine-patch block.

Ocean Waves
c.1880, Ohio
68 x 72 inches
Museum Quilts Gallery, London, England

THROUGHOUT THE NINETEENTH CENTURY, the combination of indigo-dyed blue and white was a popular color preference for both pieced and appliqué quilts, as well as for woven coverlets. Indigo was introduced to Europe in the mid-sixteenth century from India, and replaced the extremely difficult blue dye technique using woad. It remained in use as the main source of blue dye until 1856 when synthetic aniline dyes were invented.

Inspired by the ceaseless motion of the sea, this optical quilt is a shifting vision of indigo and white. It is a difficult piecing exercise and is a testimonial to the maker's sewing ability. Several thousand, one-inch triangles have been sewn together to create the dark grid that represents the ocean waves.

THE BASKET, WHETHER APPLIQUÉD LIKE THE ELABORATE, flower filled baskets of the Baltimore Album quilts or pieced into a simple, geometric shape, remains a popular quilt pattern. When the fashion for appliqué and central medallion quilts was replaced by pieced block quilts, the basket was adapted and simplified into various geometric configurations. The patterns which emerged—Flowerpots, Basket of Chips, Cake Stand and Grape Basket —are all pieced using a different arrangement of small and large triangles.

   This crib quilt uses a popular mid-nineteenth-century color scheme of chrome yellow set against a dark indigo background. The brightness of color, and the tiny floral design on the fabrics, give the quilt a charming Provençal quality.

Flowerpots
c.1880, Pennsylvania
40 x 41 inches
From the Martha Jackson Collection, Vermont

$\mathscr{T}$HE ORIGIN OF THIS HIGHLY EVOCATIVE PATTERN NAME IS UNKNOWN. It conjures up pictures of hope brought by the morning sun streaming through a window, of the arrival of peace or simply of a bird flapping on a window pane. The theme of birds continues in the Flying Geese border.

Names for quilt patterns draw inspiration from any number of sources—nature, politics, events, daily life, folk motifs. Until the nineteenth century, pattern names were not documented and were passed orally from one quiltmaker to the next. In time, their origins were confused, lost or re-invented to suit the maker.

Dove at the Window
c.1880, western Pennsylvania
80 x 94 inches
Museum Quilts Gallery, London, England

*D*URING THE NINETEENTH CENTURY, women brought their quilts into the political arena. They championed the causes of temperance and women's rights and decorated their quilts with slogans and portraits of their favorite candidates. This quilt celebrates the 1880 Republican Presidential campaign led by James A. Garfield and Chester A. Arthur.

A twenty-inch, commemorative bandanna of the two candidates is used as the central medallion. A design of alternating dark and light triangles surrounds the portraits. Each large triangle is composed of twenty-five smaller ones. The dark triangles and the border are cut from a rich array of turkey red dyed fabrics.

Garfield and Arthur
c.1880, Pennsylvania
84 x 84 inches
From the Shelly Zegart Collection, Kentucky

*T*HE NAME OF THIS TYPE OF QUILT REFERS to its log-like contruction. Narrow strips of cloth are assembled onto a foundation cloth in the same way that logs are layered in the building of a cabin. The pattern is built up around a small square, usually red and supposedly representing the hearth. The placement of light and dark strips within each block and the arrangement of the blocks creates the pattern. There are at least six different variations of the Log Cabin design—Court House Steps, Barn Raising, Streak of Lightning, Straight Furrows and Pineapple.

Log Cabin, Light and Dark Variation
c.1880, Kentucky
70 x 82 inches
Museum Quilts Gallery, London, England

$\mathcal{I}$T IS HARD TO BELIEVE THAT THIS EXTRAORDINARILY MODERN looking quilt was made in rural America in the latter half of the nineteenth century. Its sophisticated use of color and graphic strength puts it in league with the best of the abstract modernists.

The quilt has been made using just four blocks. Each chrome yellow quarter has been outlined with a sawtooth border. This gives the quilt its duality. When the yellow shapes dominate, it looks like a moon in a night sky with its four phases in each corner, and when the blue dominates, it appears to be an elaborate keyhole.

Sunburst
c.1880, Kentucky
67 x 77 inches
From the Shelly Zegart Collection, Kentucky

THIS DAZZLING BRITISH PATCHWORK QUILT is composed of a rich and colorful selection of woven silk and satin dress fabrics. Some three thousand tiny triangles have been used to create the mosaic centerpiece. The diamond pattern around the centerpiece has been achieved by turning the small pieced squares on-point and then dividing each with sashing strips and posts. The sashing and the tiny square corner posts define the shape of each block.

The predominance of saturated pink, purple and magenta fabrics indicates that the fabrics used in making this quilt have been colored with aniline dyes. Aniline, a coal tar derivative, was discovered by chance in 1856 by an English chemist, William Henry Perkin. It provided the late nineteenth century with a new range of colorfast fabrics in mauves, reds, greens and browns.

The quilt is finished with borders of yellow taffeta and brown satin. These were popular late Victorian colors. It has been very simply machine-quilted in a broad cross-hatch pattern. The qualitative differences between the piecing and quilting suggest that the quilting may have been done by another person.

English Silk Patchwork
c.1870, England
98 x 106 inches
Courtesy The Antique Textile Company, London, England

$\mathcal{T}$HE SPOOL IS A POPULAR NINETEENTH-CENTURY scrap pattern, and its name still lies close to the heart of any active needlewoman. Quiltmakers spend many years collecting fabric scraps, and it would have taken the maker of this quilt a considerable amount of time to accumulate the 2,300 pieces needed to complete the design.

In the nineteenth century when women of every age and class sewed, the scrap bags would have been common to all households. Into it went leftover dress and furnishing fabrics and worn garments. Women exchanged their scraps and passed on their collection to their children and grandchildren. The fact that a quilt might be made up of fabrics that had been stored over generations can make their dating rather difficult.

Spools
c.1890, Kansas
60 x 74 inches
Museum Quilts Gallery, London, England

*T*HE CRAZY QUILT WAS A CURIOUS AND FANCIFUL VICTORIAN INVENTION. Rather than geometric pieces of cotton or wool, irregular scraps of velvet, brocade, silk, satin and taffeta were used, often from worn garments and old furnishing fabrics.

The idea of piecing together fabric scraps dates back to the origins of patchwork when necessity dictated the haphazard quality of the finished item. But it is doubtful whether this utilitarian memory in any way influenced the extraordinary Crazy Quilt phenomenon that swept across America and England.

Several factors help to explain the avid pursuit of new needlework ideas. Firstly, the aesthetic philosophies of the Decorative Arts Movement urged that everyday objects be imbued with beauty and decorative detail, as well as being clearly functional. Secondly, the Japanese exhibits at the Centennial Exhibition in Philadelphia caused a sensation, and thousands of visitors returned home inspired by Eastern asymmetrical design principles. Using these two concepts as a springboard, and encouraged by media which promoted the oriental look, the fashion for things "crazy" took off.

This splendid figurative crazy quilt is made up of 12 blocks, each a rich and artful composition. They have been decorated with examples of the Victorian preoccupation for things new and exotic. Natural history abounds in the shape of embroidered leaves, shells and animals. The science of flight features as air balloons, a mourning hair-brooch is stitched onto one block and the embroidered words Velours de Paris appear as a souvenir piece of fabric.

Figurative Crazy Quilt
c.1890, USA
86 x 73 inches
From the Betsy Nimock Collection, Missouri

$\mathcal{N}$INETY MINIATURE BLOCKS SURROUND THE CENTRAL Hearts and Hand motif. Each block has a story to tell and the two blocks with coffins bring a note of sorrow to what is otherwise a colorful display of pattern and technique.

This quilt incorporates both hand and machine sewing. The arrival of the sewing machine in 1850 contributed to the growth of quiltmaking. Hailed as one of the greatest labor-saving devices, manufacturers of the domestic sewing machine promised to free women from unnecessary toil. Before its arrival, hand sewing might have consumed more hours of a woman's day than any other single task. By the 1890s the sewing machine had become an established domestic fixture and the majority of quilts made from this date would have been machine pieced. Being able to piece quickly and accurately inspired quiltmakers to be more adventurous, and certainly more prolific.

Hearts and Hand Sampler
c.1890, Pennsylvania
86 x 70 inches
From the Rowland and Eleanor Bingham Miller Collection. Photo courtesy Shelly Zegart

A STRIP QUILT, OR "STRIPPY" AS IT IS COLLOQUIALLY KNOWN IN THE NORTH OF ENGLAND, is made from long, patterned or plain alternating bands of fabric. This type of quilt design was particularly popular in Wales and in the northern counties of England between 1860 and 1930.

The large uninterrupted areas of fabric and the simplicity of design encouraged elaborate displays of intricate quilting. This Welsh quilt, dramatically pieced in scarlet and blue wool, is a masterpiece of the quilting technique. It has been exquisitely stitched with a catalog of challenging patterns—leaves, roses, spirals, medallions and waves.

Welsh Strippy in Red and Blue
c.1890, Dyfed, Wales
78 x 84 inches
From the Ron Simpson Collection, London, England

TRADITIONALLY, WELSH QUILTERS EXPRESS A PREFERENCE for dramatic but simple geometric designs in strong and saturated colors—red, magenta, purple, indigo, green and black. In sharp contrast to their plain and simple living, their quilts are an exuberant celebration of color and fanciful quilting patterns. The anonymous maker of this nineteenth-century quilt achieves an extraordinary modernity with her bold use of color and simple repeating star pattern. It would have provided a great splash of color and warmth to the spartan interior of a Welsh stone cottage. The quilt, pieced from woolen cloth, has been stitched with an elaborate overall feather design.

Welsh Variable Star
c.1900, Carmarthen, Wales
80 x 80 inches
From the Ron Simpson Collection, London, England

*T*HIS UNUSUAL SIGNATURE QUILT IS AN EMBROIDERED historical document which, like a family tree, lists the members of the Rairigh family back to their ancestor, William Rairigh. Embroidered at the top of the quilt are the following words—"These are the descendants of William Rairigh through one hundred years 1796 - 1896." Some one hundred family members have been embroidered onto this pieced quilt of plain black cotton. Catharine Clark has used a variety of embroidery stitches to record her family tree.

Signature quilts were very popular in America in the last half of the nineteenth century and were usually made for presentation to departing or retiring prominent community members or to raise money. For fundraising purposes, a fee would be charged to have one's name recorded, either embroidered or inscribed with an indelible pen onto the quilt. The finished quilt would then be raffled or donated to a charitable cause.

Signature Quilt
signed and dated: "Catharine L. Clark March 30 1896," USA
84 x 87 inches
From the Shelly Zegart Collection, Kentucky

These are the names of the descendents of William Rairigh through one hundred years. 1796 . 1896

William Rairigh 1796
Barby Rairigh
Moses Rairigh
Evina Mealey 1821
George Mealy
Jesse Rairigh 1823
Mary Rairigh

Elizabeth Rairigh 1809
Catharine Clark 1841
George Clark 1829
Wm M Rairigh 1848
Mary M Rang 1853
Elizabeth Rairigh 183?
Angaline Holobaugh 1858

S G Rairie 1850
Carrie Rairie 1849
Ursula Weamer 1869
Albert Weamer 1857
Ina F Weamer 1889
Edna B Weamer 1891
Thomas Holobaugh

R F Miller 1871
Lizzy Miller 1876
Oran McMiller
G C Wadding
Edith Wadding
Pearl Massena
A E Massena

A F Rairigh 1852
C E Rairigh 1854
Leonard Rairigh 1878
Winona A Rairigh 1876
Frank Mealy
Tillie Mealy
Lester Mealy

Elisabeth Hill 1854
James Hill
Nancy Lilly
James Lilly
Oliver Mealy
Olive Mealy
Murl Mealy

Carrie Beary
John Beary
W L Rairigh
Julia Rairigh
O C Rairigh
L M Rairigh
March 30 1896

Made by Catharine L Clark

Rairigh
Aldo
Mary
Vienna
Bolda
Violet
Homer
Sidney
Lauisa C
Lucy B
William
Miles
Sarah
Cora
Alice
Clara
Olive
Homer
Harold
Iven
Joseph
Annie
Cloyd
Lorence
Cornelius
Hill
Effie
Jesse
Arthur
Lorence
Olive
Maggie

Pastel Diamond in a Square
c.1900, Wales
84 x 110 inches
From the Ron Simpson Collection, London, England

THIS MEDALLION QUILT HAS BEEN PIECED FROM A SELECTION of warm-toned, possibly home-dyed woolen fabrics and includes a mixture of tweeds, flannel and suiting materials. The quilt is constructed of a series of borders around the central Diamond in a Square motif. Some are just simple strips of cloth and others are pieced, like the Flying Geese and Sawtooth patterns. The quilting is functional, simply following the outline of the pieced shapes, and indicates that it was made as a utility quilt for everyday purposes.

Spools in a Square
c.1900, Wales
96 x 96 inches
From the Ron Simpson Collection, London, England

*B*EAUTIFUL, EARTH-TONED WOOLEN FABRICS HAVE BEEN SEWN TOGETHER to create this medallion quilt. A one-patch brickwork pattern frames the centerpiece of four spools. The saturated purple fabrics used in this quilt were extremely popular with Welsh quilters. Unlike the pastel medallion quilt on the previous page, this piece has been beautifully quilted with circles, spirals and wave patterns, and was intended as a "best" quilt.

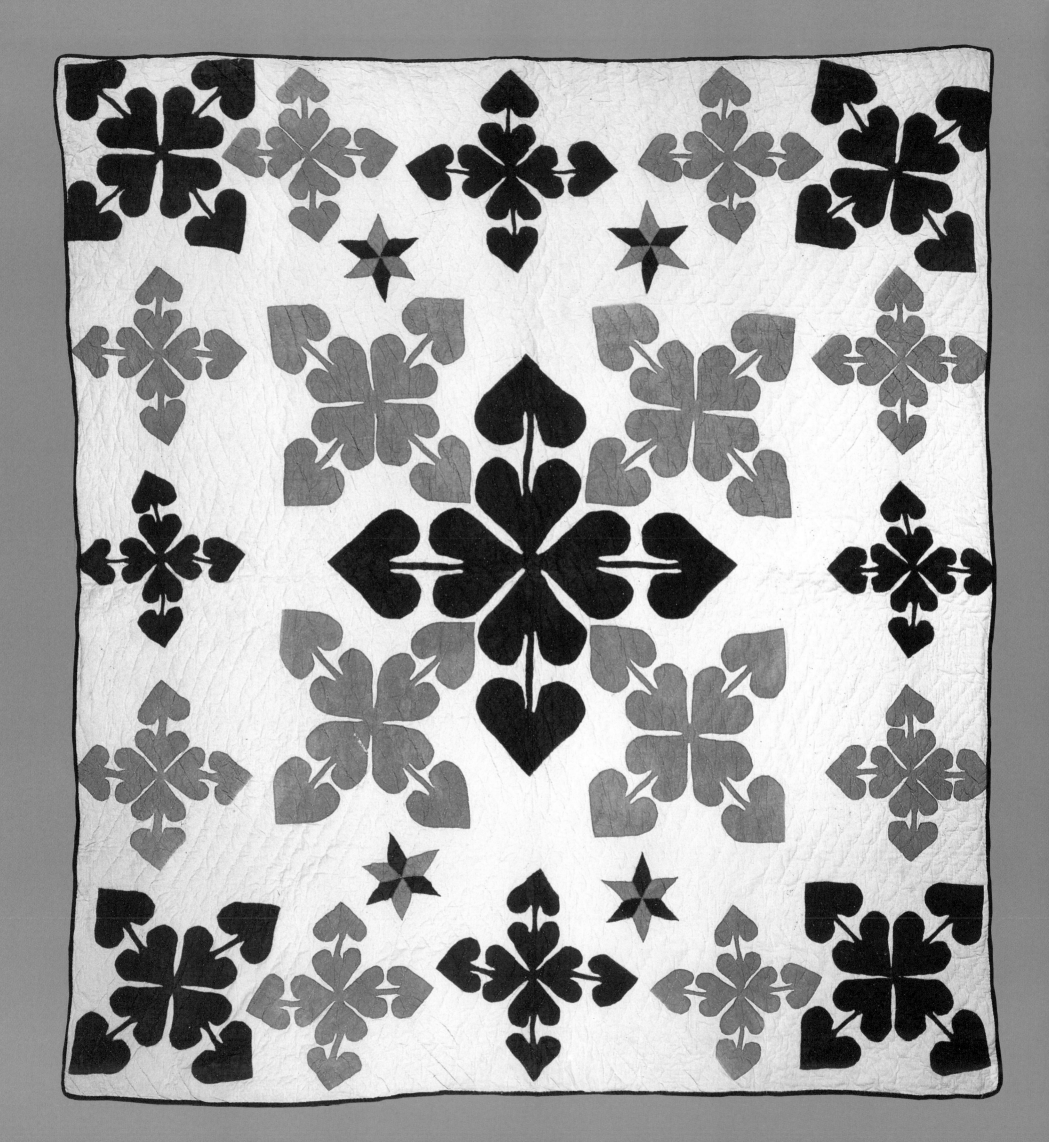

*T*HIS EXUBERANT QUILT IN PATRIOTIC COLORS OF RED, WHITE AND BLUE was made using a paper-cutting method, popular among the Pennsylvanian German communities. The fabric is folded to precise specifications and then cut so that a perfectly symmetrical pattern is formed.

Using the heart as a single motif, the maker has made a clever arrangement to create a clover shape. No doubt she was following the old adage of "where there is love there is luck." A careful and simple symmetry is achieved in the design by setting the large leitmotif on point and surrounding it by smaller versions in a square formation.

Love and Luck
c.1900, Vermont
70 x 80 inches
Museum Quilts Gallery, London, England

*T*HIS SIMPLE DESIGN IS CREATED BY SEWING BANDS of alternating patterned and plain triangles. The name Pyramids refers to the triangle shape used: a short base-line triangle.

In this quilt of Victorian silks, the black triangles vie for dominance with identically sized triangles pieced from narrow colorful strips. When the quilt is viewed vertically, the pattern appears as a zig-zag basket weave. In a horizontal position, the black faced triangles appear three-dimensional, with the striped triangles providing the illusion of depth.

A distinctly visible and poorly executed seamline, three-quarters of the way down the quilt, suggests that either the quilt has been extended, or that part of it, possibly because of damage, has been cut away and the remaining two sections sewn back together.

Pyramids
c.1900, USA
51 x 86 inches
From the Besty Nimock Collection, Colorado

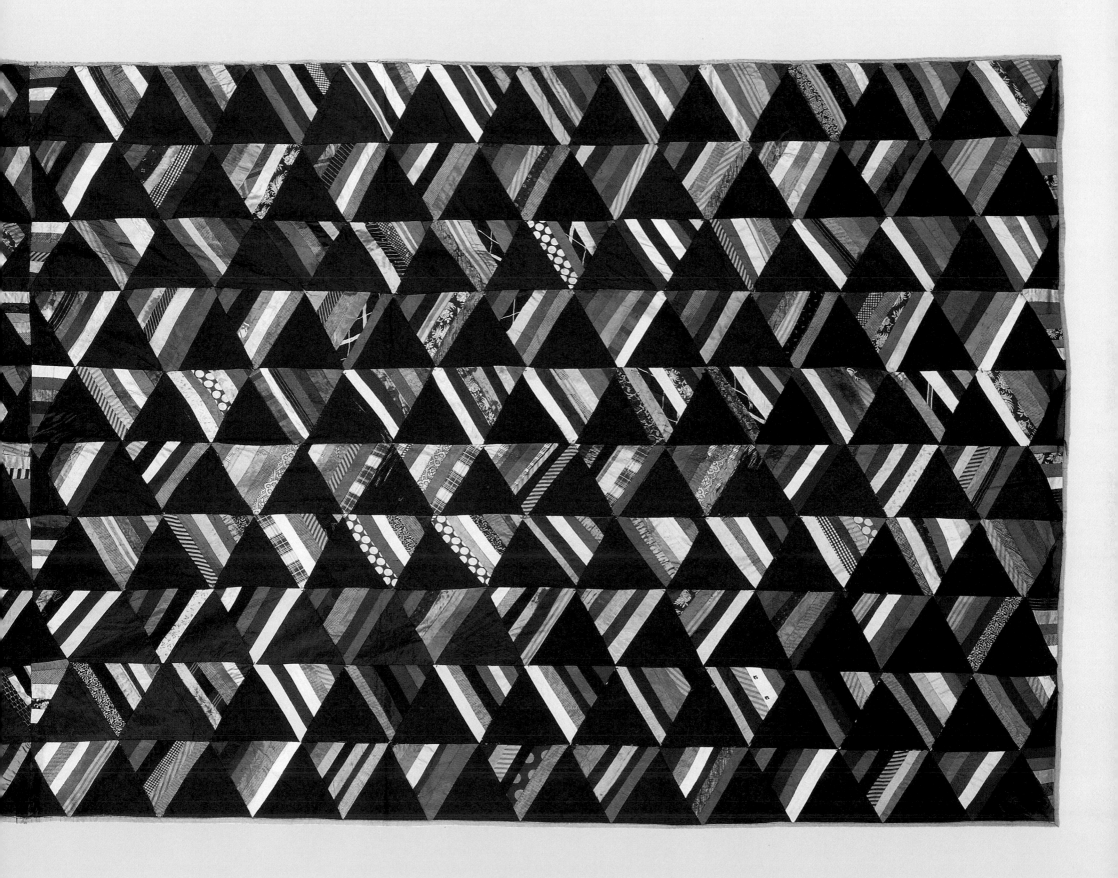

As a quilting pattern the feather motif dates back to the seventeenth century, and there are many examples of it used in garments and coverlets. The earliest date-inscribed example of this design as an appliqué quilt is dated 1818.

The Princess Feather—of which there are many variations such as the feather wreath, the running feather, feather with flowers, feathers as the central medallion—is an elegant pattern that demands a large expanse in order to be visually effective. This version, worked in indigo blue and turkey red on a white background, is simply composed of just four large blocks.

Turkey red was a successful colorfast dye for producing a distinctive scarlet color. The complicated method of obtaining the dye from madder root and alzarin was brought to Europe from the East in the eighteenth century. The process was kept secret. In 1785 the Scottish dyehouse Dale and Macintosh announced in a national newspaper: "Dale and Macintosh...are just begun to dye cotton yarn Turkey Red for the Manufacturers at large, at 3s (shillings) per lb weight."

Princess Feather Variation
c.1900, Schuylkill County, Pennsylvania
78 x 80 inches
Museum Quilts Gallery, London, England

A WHOLE-CLOTH, AS ITS NAME SUGGESTS, IS A QUILTED spread made up of just one length of fabric. It is popular with quilters who want to draw attention to their quilting skills. On this paisley patterned quilt you need to look at the reverse side to admire the quilting, for on the top it has been lost in the intricate pattern of the cotton print. The uninterrupted quilting patterns of diamonds, spirals and half-circles are clearly visible on the brown, glazed cotton backing.

Wales has a long tradition of quilting, which dates back to the sixteenth century. It fell into decline in the twentieth century, partly due to the introduction of these decorative printed cotton fabrics which concealed the quilting.

Paisley Whole-cloth
c.1900, Wales
74 x 84 inches
From the Ron Simpson Collection, London, England

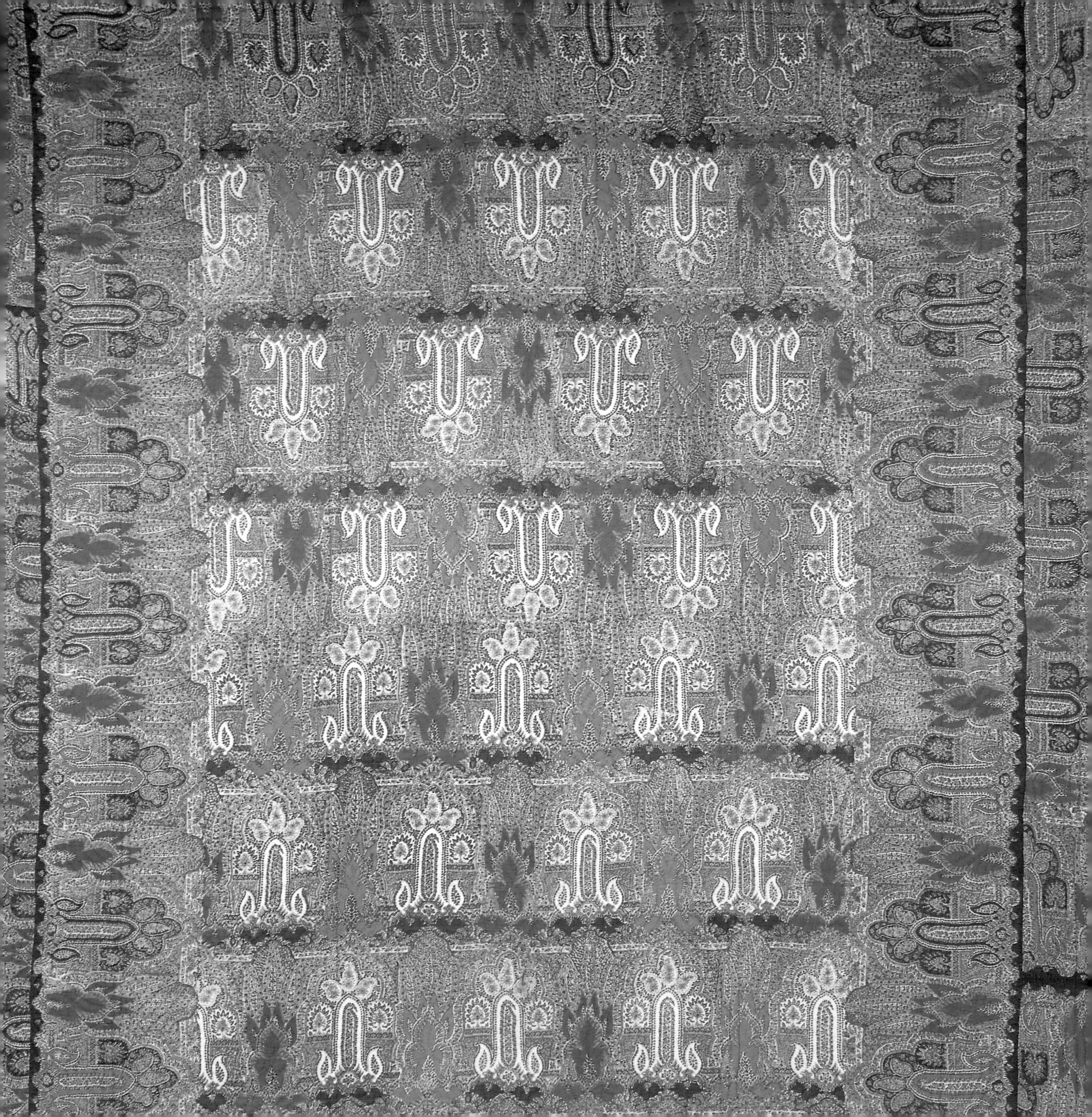

*A*LTHOUGH DEEPLY DEVOUT, THE AMISH QUILTER used few patterns with an obvious religious connection. The Crown of Thorns is a rare exception to this rule.

Amish quilt patterns may have specific pictorial names, but they are pieced using abstract geometric shapes. Pictorial realism in a quilt top is forbidden by the Amish church. The majority of Amish quilts are assembled using basic geometric shapes—squares, diamonds, rectangles and triangles. Unlike Diamond in a Square, which is based on a variation of the central medallion style, Crown of Thorns is a simple block construction of squares and triangles.

Amish Crown of Thorns
*c.*1920, Iowa
72 x 72 inches
Museum Quilts Gallery, London, England

THE DIAMOND IN A SQUARE IS A POPULAR AMISH DESIGN. A square within a square is an abstract development of the central medallion style of quilt. This fine wool quilt is a wonderful example of the awe-inspiring color preferences of the Amish quilters in Pennsylvania. They use a palette of saturated blues, magenta, purples and greens. Amish communities in Ohio and the Midwest have a brighter palette. But common to all three regions is a refusal to introduce printed fabrics into their work.

The simple piecing of this design allows for large areas of elaborate quilting. In contrast to their very sober lifestyle, the Amish needlewomen embellish their quilts with intricate and ornate quilting patterns. Realistic representation is permissible in quilting only—fruits, feathers, flowers, wreaths, scrolls, stars, baskets, circles and graceful curves abound. Often a single quilt may be stitched with four or more quilting patterns. Within the stringent physical and social constraints of the Amish way of life, the women have found an acceptable way of endowing their needlework with individuality.

Amish Diamond in a Square
c. 1930, Lancaster County, Pennsylvania
78 x 78 inches
Museum Quilts Gallery, London, England

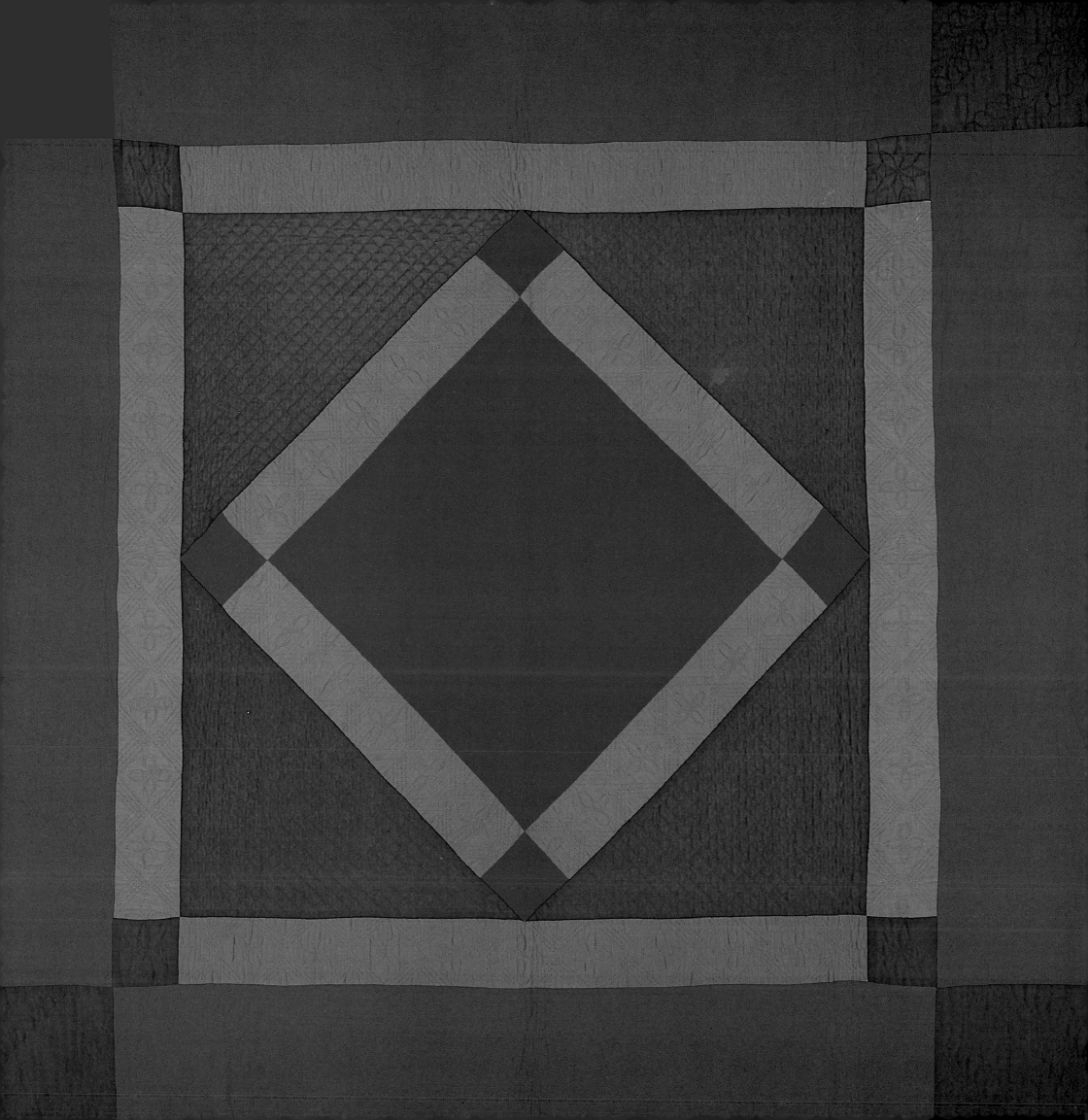

Amish Log Cabin, Barn Raising Variation
c.1900, Pennsylvania
76 x 80 inches
Museum Quilts Gallery, London, England

ANOTHER POPULAR DESIGN AMONG AMISH QUILTMAKERS is the Log Cabin, of which there are many variations. The design is made using light and dark colored strips sewn around a central square onto a foundation block. The placement of light and dark dictates the resulting pattern. For instance, by arranging the strips in diagonals of light and dark, the Barn Raising and Straight Furrows patterns are created.

In this quilt, the Barn Raising pattern is achieved by placing four red corners together to make the central square. This is then surrounded by blocks with brown sides facing the center square.

Amish Bear's Paw
c.1920, Ohio
72 x 82 inches
Museum Quilts Gallery, London, England

*B*right colors on dark grounds characterize much of the work of Ohio Amish quilters. This inspired piece is beautifully proportioned and finely quilted.

Bear's Paw is the traditional name for several patterns worked by quilters in western Pennsylvania and Ohio, where bear tracks were a common sight. The same basic pattern also goes by the names Duck's Foot in the Mud, Hands of Friendship and Hands All Around.

THE CONSTRUCTION OF A CRAZY QUILT DIFFERS from that of a pieced block. It is built up by sewing irregular shaped pieces onto a calico foundation. The pieces are overlapped and invisibly stitched down. The fun of ornamentation then begins—the shapes are embellished with elaborate embroidery stitches, ribbons, buttons, charms and hand-painted motifs.

Bearing motifs of the American flag and the Red Cross, this quilt was made to celebrate the end of World War I. Fifteen randomly pieced blocks have been decorated with a wealth of embroidered detail. Farmyard birds and animals have been created with a variety of difficult embroidery stitches, which include chevron stitch, feather stitch, herringbone and chain stitch.

World War I Crazy Quilt
1918, Minneapolis, Minnesota
63 x 82 inches
Private Collection

The tree is a popular motif in quiltmaking, and first appears on eighteenth-century palampores and chintz cut-out appliqué (broderie perse) quilts. The decorative flowering tree offered new settlers a sense of domestic comfort in what was, for many, a great and frightening wilderness. By the nineteenth century, settlers faced the natural world with confidence. They had domesticated the massive white pine that once filled their forefathers with awe and longing for the neat woods of Europe. It provided them with life-sustaining materials—timber for their log cabins and fuel for their fire, as well as furniture, cutlery, turpentine, paint and tar.

Other variations on the triangular-shaped tree are Tree of Temptation, Temperance Tree, Pine Tree and Live Oak Tree.

This quilt has been pieced using alternating diamonds of pastel blue and white calico with coarse denim for the trees.

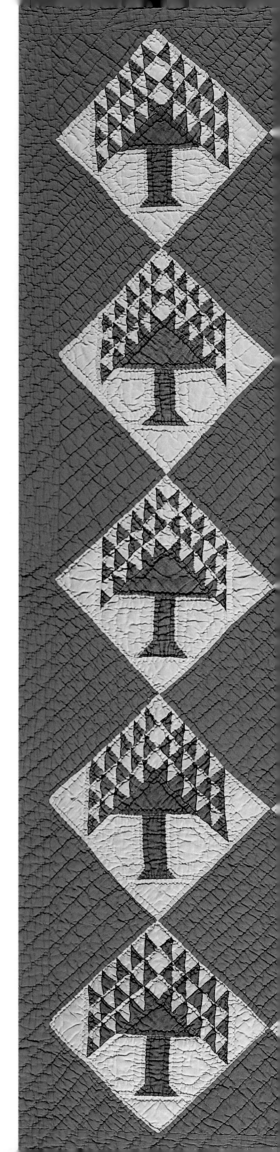

Tree of Life
1911, Blue Ridge Mountains, North Carolina
62 x 74 inches
Museum Quilts Gallery, London, England

$\mathcal{Q}$UILT PATTERN NAMES ARE NUMEROUS, changeable, and frequently influenced by the environment and circumstance of the maker. For instance, this pattern was known in the nineteenth century as Rocky Mountain Road and Crown of Thorns, reflecting a time when life was hard and hazardous for the early settlers, and religion provided them with a source of comfort. The name New York Beauty is resonant with the buoyancy of the twentieth century and the new prosperous quilt industry. Commercial forces demanded a new vocabulary of modern and optimistic quilt pattern names.

New York Beauty
c.1920, Michigan
96 x 80 inches
Museum Quilts Gallery, London, England

*F*ROM AFAR THIS HIGHLY DECORATIVE QUILT TOP looks like a tablet of hieroglyphics from a lost civilization. On a foundation of black woolen cloth the maker has created a fascinating network of interlocking shapes. Using colorful silk threads she has freely embroidered the throw with an intricate topstitch. The improvisational quality of the embroidery is harnessed by dividing bands of silk ribbon.

Crazy work was not exclusively the domain of quilts. The delicacy of these works made them more suitable as decorative throws, screens, curtains, tea cosies and mantelpiece scarves. The fashion for crazy quilts had passed by the late 1880s but, as this quilt testifies, the desire for high decoration will always remain.

The forty-eight stars on the small silk flags help us to date the quilt somewhere after 1912 when Arizona entered the Union as the 48th State and before 1959 when Alaska became the 49th State.

Patriotic Crazy Quilt
20th century, USA
68 x 56 inches
Museum Quilts Gallery, London, England

$\mathcal{U}$NTIL THE TWENTIETH CENTURY SEWING WAS AN ESSENTIAL skill learned by all girls. The rudiments of "plain" sewing were taught at home as soon as girls could comfortably wield a needle, and at school sewing was part of the curriculum. Nineteenth-century sample books from elementary schools prove that children were taught to oversew, buttonhole and hem, and that these techniques were frequently practised in making a patchwork quilt.

In the center of May Bowen's delightful quilt is a medallion of stitched canvas work, portraying a woman milking a green cow with pink polka-dots. She has surrounded it with a simple one-patch, brickwork design, pieced from a selection of plain woolens and tweeds. The pieces have been feather-stitched in red, white and blue cotton thread and simply quilted with a diagonal pattern.

One-patch with Needlepoint
made by May Bowen, 1915, Wales
55 x 68 inches
From the Ron Simpson Collection, London, England

THIS STRIKINGLY SIMPLE, GEOMETRIC PATTERN IS A VARIATION of the Bars design. Whether inspired by ploughed furrows or the neat rows of vegetable beds tended by a rural community, this pattern is a particular favorite of Mennonite, as well as Welsh and Amish, quilters.

Based on the Biblical story about Joseph and his coat of many colors, this quilt is a visual feast of color and quilting patterns. Pieced in narrow columns of plain cotton fabric, each of the seven different bands has been quilted with a different pattern—chains, diamonds, cable, zig-zag, feather and a meandering Greek pattern.

Mennonite Joseph's Coat
c.1920, Pennsylvania
70 x 78 inches
Museum Quilts Gallery, London, England

PROVENANCE HAS IT THAT THIS QUILT WAS MADE AS A WEDDING GIFT for the marriage of members of two prominent families from Philadelphia. It is an unusual choice of subject matter for a bridal quilt. Usually these are album type quilts appliquéd with floral and symbolic motifs of union and happiness. This quilt depicts the moment of terrible realization when Adam and Eve come to understand the significance of biting the Apple.

It has been appliquéd in the charming pastel colors that were so popular with quiltmakers in the early part of the twentieth century. Prominent are the "Pastoral" colors of rose pink, lilac, copen blue, nile green and dark green. These colors of quality cotton sateen appeared in a range called "Pastoral Cloth." They were considerably more expensive than the standard cottons used for quiltmaking, and yet despite the effects of the Depression this expensive cotton cloth was the staple fabric choice for fancy quilts.

The Garden of Eden
1926, Philadelphia
73 x 81 inches
From the Martha Jackson Collection, Vermont

$\mathcal{G}$RANDMOTHER'S FLOWER GARDEN IS A ONE-PATCH DESIGN constructed from hexagonal shapes. Along with Dresden Plate and Double Wedding Ring, it remains one of the most popular patterns of the twentieth century. When hexagons are simply sewn together in rows, the emerging pattern is a honeycomb (see the quilt on the back of the jacket). Grandmother's Flower Garden evolved from this simple pattern.

To create the garden, a mid-toned hexagon is used for the center. Then, this is surrounded by one or more rings of flower-colored prints, a ring of green for the foliage and a ring of white to represent the path.

In this garden, the hexagons have been worked to create elongated diamond shapes. By resting your eye on the quilt, Grandmother's Garden begins to be transformed—a blue star emerges and then a pattern of building blocks takes shape. This optical effect is called an illusion of pattern and periodic structure.

Grandmother's Flower Garden
made by Dena Williams
c.1930, Wright City, Missouri
72 x 96 inches
Museum Quilts Gallery, London, England

$\mathcal{C}$OMMERCIAL PATTERN HOUSES MADE A SIGNIFICANT CONTRIBUTION to the twentieth-century quilt revival that took place between 1920 and 1930. The wealth of attractive new patterns, along with their easy availability through magazines, newspapers and mail order houses, inspired many women to make quilts. This highly amusing alphabet quilt may have been made from one of the many quilt patterns which were published weekly in newspapers, one block at a time. It has only sixteen different letters, with the D and O repeated. This peculiar choice of letters suggests that the maker was engaged in some game or word play with the three boys for whom it was made. From the names stitched onto children's building blocks, we can assume that Bruce, David and Steven were the happy recipients of this charming nursery quilt.

Characters from nursery rhymes appear around the four sides of the sage green border: Little Boy Blue sleeps in the corn surrounded by the Three Little Pigs and a host of farmyard animals; Humpty Dumpty smiles from his wall; and the Cat plays the fiddle while the Cow jumps over the moon watched by a family of bears.

Alphabet Quilt
c.1930, USA
70 x 90 inches
Museum Quilts Gallery, London, England

*F*LORAL APPLIQUÉ QUILTS REACHED THEIR HEIGHT OF POPULARITY in the USA during the 1930s, when thousands of patterns were published. The appliqué technique is simply the laying of one piece of fabric onto another, securing it by stitching it down with minute stitches so as to appear invisible. This is the oldest form of quiltmaking and has been used over centuries by Chinese, Indian, Middle Eastern and European civilizations.

This gorgeous pastel quilt is a great needlework achievement. Each tiny appliqué flower, leaf and bird attempts a botanical accuracy, and the quilting work is of an exceptionally high standard. The quilt is meticulously designed so that the central floral ring will lie on top of the bed leaving the sides hanging to best display the exquisite quilting. This design was inspired by a quilt made by Arsinoe Kelsey Bowen of Maryland in 1857, and made famous by later copies and adaptations quilted by Rose G. Kretsinger and Pine Eisfeller.

Paradise Garden Appliqué
signed and dated: "A Y," 1935
Cape Cod, Massachusetts
93 x 101 inches
From the Shelly Zegart Collection, Kentucky

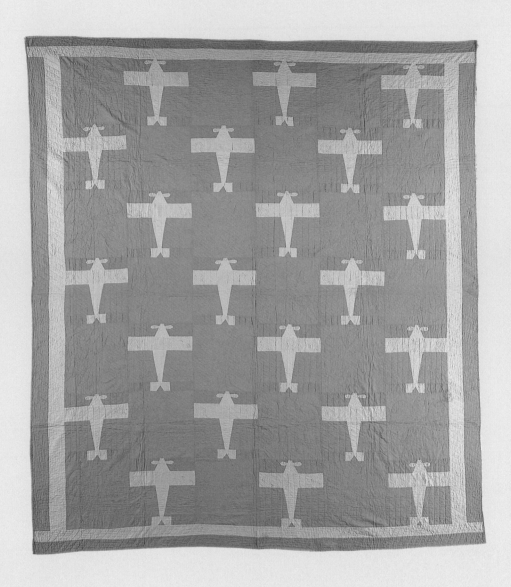

Charles Lindbergh Commemorative Quilt
1930, USA
76 x 83 inches
Museum Quilts Gallery, London, England

*T*HE RUSH OF TECHNOLOGICAL ACHIEVEMENTS IN THE TWENTIETH CENTURY was cause for celebration, and the excitement generated a host of new quilt patterns.

The solo flight of Charles Lindbergh in his monoplane, the *Spirit of St. Louis*, across the Atlantic in 1927 caught the popular imagination, and he affectionately became known as the "Lone Eagle." Commercial pattern makers were quick to produce a quilt design to celebrate America's new aviation hero. Twenty-one single engine airplanes in white calico on a saffron yellow ground have been simply pieced and finished with an appliquéd propeller. Each alternate block has been quilted with the Lone Eagle pattern.

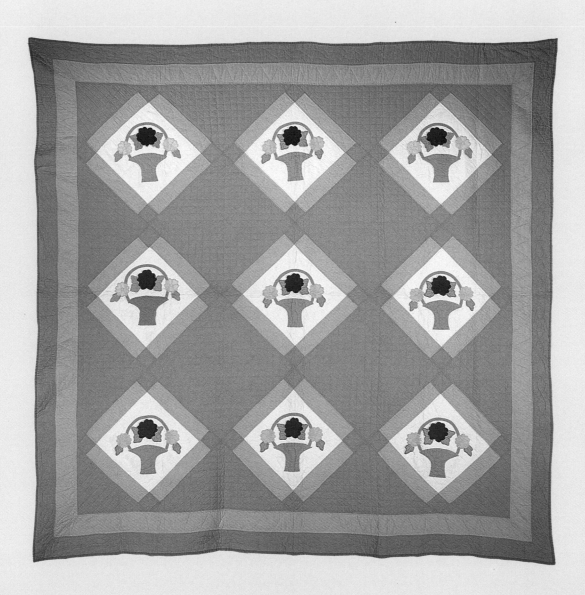

Flower Baskets
c.1940, Michigan
82 x 82 inches
Museum Quilts Gallery, London, England

THIS SIMPLE, SPRINGTIME QUILT HAS BEEN EXECUTED in the fashionable pastel shades of the 1940s. Nine charming floral baskets, each set in a window, are framed by strips of delicate pink shirting fabric. The quilt has been playfully constructed using blocks set on point, resulting in shapes that constantly shift emphasis. Large blue diamonds vie with smaller white shapes for dominance.

Three different quilting patterns have been used to stitch the quilt layers together—cable, zig-zag and cross-hatch. The appliqué details have been highlighted with a buttonhole stitch embroidered in contrasting colored thread.

*T*HE TWENTIETH CENTURY SAW A PROLIFERATION of pieced and appliqué patterns inspired by everyday objects. While the nineteenth-century quilters abstracted reality into geometric patterns, the twentieth-century quilters pursued a new realism. No object was too banal to immortalize in fabric—umbrellas, shoes, cups, kittens, cars, turtles, trolley cars, dogs and donkeys. In their use of repetition of mundane objects, these light-hearted quilts can be seen as forerunners of Pop Art.

The Sailors quilt was probably made in the 1940s for a loved one serving in the United States Navy. The vivid solid lavender fabric used for the background blocks only became possible with the arrival of synthetic dyes in the early years of the twentieth century. Before this, purple fabrics were not widely used as they were not colorfast. Unless stored in darkness, they faded to pink or brown.

Sailors
c.1940, USA
84 x 66 inches
Museum Quilts Gallery, London, England

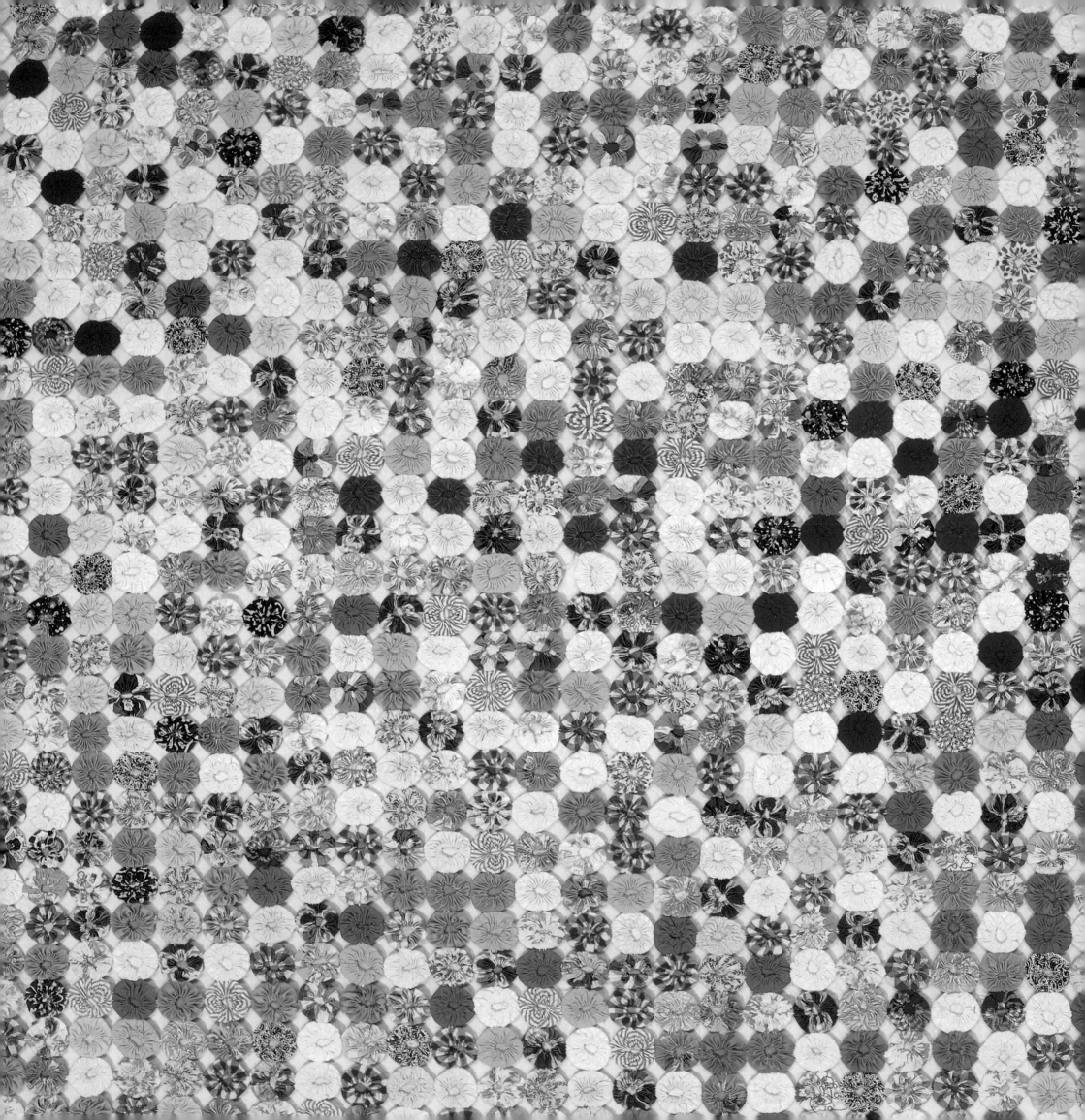

*T*HIS NOVELTY QUILT IS A MODERN ADAPTATION of the English Suffolk puff quilt. It is not a true quilt in that it does not consist of three layers of fabric sewn together. A yo-yo quilt is made entirely of small circles of cloth. The edge of each circle is turned in, gathered with thread and fastened, so that the resulting medallion is smooth on one side and puckered on the other. The separate medallions are joined either in a specific design or in a random way reminiscent of scrap quilts. This form of decorative quilt was particularly popular between the years 1920 and 1930.

Yo-yo Quilt
c.1930, USA
62 x 84 inches
Museum Quilts Gallery, London, England

Acknowledgments

Grateful thanks are due to the following private collectors, curators, museums and organizations who contributed their quilts and expertise to this publication: Rowland and Eleanor Bingham Miller; David Bartels; Sheila Betterton; Jean Bowden and Anne Channon, "Chawton," Jane Austen's House, Alton, Hampshire, England; Elizabeth Conran and Joanna Hashagen, The Bowes Museum, Barnard Castle, Co. Durham, England; Shelagh Ford, The American Museum, Claverton Manor, Nr Bath, Avon, England; Sarah Franklyn and Judy Wentworth, The Antique Textile Company, P.O. Box 2800, London, England; Aly Goodwin, Black Mountain Antique Mall, 100 Sutton Avenue, Black Mountain, North Carolina 28711; Barbara Horvath, The BAHO Quilt Gallery, Hauptgasse 38, CH-3280 Murten, Switzerland; Martha Jackson, P.O. Box 430, Middlebury, Vermont 05753; Elizabeth McCrum, Patricia McLean and Elise Taylor, The Ulster Museum, Belfast, N. Ireland; Betsy Nimock, 300 Gay Avenue, Clayton, Missouri 63105; Ron Simpson, London, England; Ulrike Telek, The Bautzen Museum, Kornmarkt 1, 02625-Bautzen, Germany; Betsey Telford and Gloria White, Rocky Mountain Quilts, 3847 Alt 6 & 24, Palisade, Colorado 81526; The Welsh Folk Museum, St. Fagans, Cardiff, Wales; Shelly Zegart, 12-Z River Hill Road, Louisville, Kentucky 40207; Museum Quilts Gallery, London, England.